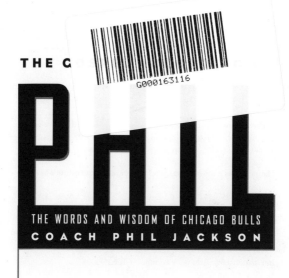

THE G

PHIL

THE WORDS AND WISDOM OF CHICAGO BULLS
COACH PHIL JACKSON

AN UNAUTHORIZED COLLECTION   COMPILED BY DAVID WHITAKER

The quotations in this book are reproduced from interviews with Phil Jackson.

01   00   99   98   97   5   4   3   2   1

Library of Congress Catalog Card Number: 97-72597
International Standard Book Number: 1-56625-086-2

Cover and interior design by Augustine Janairo Antenorcruz
Cover illustration by Dale Paracuelles

Bonus Books, Inc.   160 East Illinois Street, Chicago, Illinois 60611
Printed in the United States of America

INTRODUCTION

In his 13 years as an NBA player — most of them spent with the great New York Knicks teams of the '70s — Phil Jackson was a fierce rebounder, a brilliant defensive stopper and even a respected scoring threat. Looking and playing the part of the wayward hippie off the court, however, kept him from ever fitting the typical jock mold. To call him the Dennis Rodman of his time might be a bit of a stretch, but Jackson certainly hung tight to his individualism.

Perhaps it was his Montana roots that molded his salt-of-the-earth persona. He wore his hair long, with a beard, and revered the

Grateful Dead. He rode his bike to home games. He resigned from the Elks Club when they refused to admit black members. He spoke his mind.

So when Jackson ended his career with the New Jersey Nets in 1981, few predicted he'd make a career of coaching, let alone become one of the game's best.

The long road to the top began in Albany, NY, coaching the Patroons of the Continental Basketball Association. Although an unglamorous training ground, Jackson relished the opportunity. During a game in which the famous San Diego Chicken was hired to entertain the fans, the coach showed how seriously he took his job. When the wily mascot playfully peeked into the Patroons huddle during a crucial time-out, Jackson barked, "Get the #@*% outta here, Chicken!"

As the guiding spirit of the Chicago Bulls, however, the coach evolved into a more serene leader, infusing his practice of Zen Buddhism into an unparalleled coaching philosophy of supreme one-ness.

In just seven seasons, Jackson's humbly claimed four NBA Championships, chalked up more than 400 victories and posted the best regular season record in league history while being named the NBA's 1996 Coach of the Year. Just because he operates in the shadows of his superstar students doesn't mean he has little to say.

In fact, the man who admits lighting sticks of sagebrush to fend off bad vibes is not shy about transmitting his brain waves to the masses.

In this unauthorized compilation of inimitable quotes taken from his many encounters with the press, the coach opens up on everything from his players to his plans for the future.

Because his words stand alone, each quote is unavoidably taken out of context, leaving peaceful space for meditative reflection.

So lace up your sneakers and take a deep breath, this basketball savant shoots from the hip.

DAVID WHITAKER

"I thought
he'd be
on a farm
somewhere
growing
his own food."

That's what Walt Frazier, Jackson's
longtime teammate with the Knicks, told
U.S. NEWS AND WORLD REPORT in 1992.

• 1 •

Weight of a Feather

AFTER FOUR YEARS, Jackson was growing tired of the CBA. Concerned with the responsibility of providing for his family, he was considering law school when asked to interview for an assistant job with the Bulls. It was 1985. Sporting his shaggy beard and wearing his favorite Panama hat with a macaw's feather sticking out of the brim to a meeting with then Bulls coach Stan Albeck — and then explaining the feather's significance — probably wasn't a good idea. He didn't get the job.

"His eyes glazed over very early in the interview....And this from a guy (Albeck) who frizzes his hair."

SPORTS ILLUSTRATED. *November 11, 1991*

"I prepared myself to be an NBA head coach. I went to the CBA (1982-87), and I learned every facet of a basketball organization, top to bottom. I thought I had to know how to do everything — how to organize training camp, make trades, negotiate contracts, everything. I was wrong, but that's what I felt."

THE SPORTING NEWS. *October 30, 1989*

"I didn't want to be a 50-year-old man sitting around, still trying to become an NBA head coach."

THE SPORTING NEWS. *October 30, 1989*

"I wanted jobs, but I wanted them on my terms and I was still young enough to believe that could happen. I wasn't flaunting anything. I wore suits — don't forget I spent my whole boyhood in Sunday clothes — but, yes, I had the beard."

SPORTS ILLUSTRATED. *November 11, 1991*

"This time
I told him to
come clean,
no Panama hat....
It was
the last time
I ever
coached him."

This is what Bulls general manager
Jerry Krause told SPORTS ILLUSTRATED
in 1991 about Jackson's second job
interview with the team.

• 2 •

Gaining his Coaching Hat

JACKSON LEFT THE CBA
unsure if his next move would involve coaching. In 1987, he returned to the Bulls to interview for an assistant job under new coach Doug
Collins. He left the hat at home, and was hired.
Two years after that he took over for Collins as
head coach, and began developing a leadership
style built more on teaching than preaching.

"The coach is always a jockey. He is riding a wonderful horse and his players carry him down the racetrack. This year has been a dream year for a coach and we've had a wonderful ride up to this point."

CHICAGO TRIBUNE. *May 8, 1996*

"Maturity had something to do with our winning, and being able to blend every-one's skills, not just Michael's."

THE WALL STREET JOURNAL. *Friday, October 29, 1993*

"…There is a tenuous relationship between coaches and players and I have to have confidence in my group that they feel comfortable with the techniques I experiment with."

SAN ANTONIO EXPRESS-NEWS. *February 11, 1996*

"I found a certain level of rapport with this club because of the leadership of Michael and Scottie and their ability to motivate and keep everyone directed."

CHICAGO TRIBUNE. *June 17, 1996*

"Vested authority. If you can't win the approval of your players, you lose your job. I think the less you control them, the more innovative they can be."

VILLAGE VOICE. *April 26, 1994*

"For me, the fact that your game plan and strategies worked out — that's incidental. For me the satisfaction is that 12 guys have listened and absorbed, and found a way to band together to win."

NEW YORK TIMES MAGAZINE. *May 17, 1992*

"It's pretty straightforward stuff, really. Just relax and play."

In a 1996 interview with SPORTS ILLUSTRATED, Bulls center Bill Wennington explained how Jackson's Zen beliefs meshed with his coaching style.

· 3 ·

The Art of Coaching, and Zen Some

NOT ONLY DID JACKSON inherit Michael Jordan, perhaps the greatest player ever, but a team that was built *for* rather than around his Airness. In looking for ways to incorporate the whole of the team, Jackson relied on his own instinctual rhythms of the game — and the spiritual guidance of Zen.

"Whether on the court or off, what I call for in my people is full awareness and attention. That's really what Zen is all about — waking up and being mindful. As a team, my players have come to realize that, yes, they've got to have that kind of awareness and, yes, they've got to be extremely alert on the floor. In a sense, they become policemen of themselves, and that's really more fun for a coach to watch happen than anything else."

FORTUNE. *December 25, 1995*

"In Zen the problem is, of course, to wake up. That's what you're striving for, to get out of this dream state that we're existing in as human beings and become alert and awake for each moment that we live and approach it from that standpoint. Giving each breath significance. Basketball is very much the same: What we want is mindful, alert players, and in the process we use this tactic because this is about as close as you can come."

TV GUIDE. *Online, April 1997*

"What do you do in a Roman Catholic service? All that incense? It's mystery. Part of life is getting sucked into something with others. What we try to do with our group is breathe together, share the same space, find something outside just playing basketball on the court. This 'spiritual stuff' brings an act of community to us."

SPORTS ILLUSTRATED. *May 27, 1996*

"I just brought a guy in who did some stuff — breathing at the standing, stretching and sitting levels. Some [*players*] took to it, some rejected it. Throw enough shit at the wall, and some of it will stick."

VILLAGE VOICE. *April 26, 1994*

"I hate to schedule a practice in Washington, D.C. I'd rather take them to visit Congress."

US NEWS AND WORLD REPORT. *May 11, 1992*

"Michael Jordan called them 'Phil's head games.' I try to chide without criticism. I use sarcasm, but not deep sarcasm."

VILLAGE VOICE. *April 26, 1994*

"Phil's a lot more laid back than other coaches. He lets players be themselves. I couldn't understand that at first."

Former Bull Horace Grant described the Jackson Style in a 1994 article in the VILLAGE VOICE.

• 4 •

Be Like Phil

JACKSON'S THE FIRST TO ADMIT infusing his coaching philosophy into a team that had already proven successful was no easy task, but a process. His organic approach wasn't designed to just make others feel better about their place in the group, but to discover the true concept of team and how it relates to victory. Four championship trophies stand as testament to his bold thesis.

"Michael really likes the community aspect of basketball. He likes doing stuff with males. And the reality is, there's a certain amount of noncommunicative energy that goes on among all of us. That's spiritual - what joins us together as human beings, allows us an extraordinary group effort. Michael buys into that."

SPORTS ILLUSTRATED. *May 27, 1996*

"Even with Michael, we never saw ourselves as overwhelmingly talented, and, in fact, I think there's such a thing as a team having too many good players. I've always thought the trade that brought in Dave DeBusschere for Walt Bellamy and Howard Komives made champs of the Knicks, even though it probably reduced their overall talent level."

THE WALL STREET JOURNAL. *October 29, 1993*

"More than anything, Mike wanted us to find a way to win. He knew other guys had to score. He was willing to make that sacrifice. But he had to see it work. He had to have something to hang his hat on."

SPORTS ILLUSTRATED. *May 27, 1996*

[*on his relationship with his players*]

"It is unique in some ways, and not because they think I just smoked dope, went to parties and wore blue jeans and work shirts. There's been a lot of exchange of ideas here. We don't let things pass without talking about the whole of life, whether it's a discussion on Martin Luther King, Jr. Day or a trip to Senator [*Bill*] Bradley's office when we're playing the Bullets."

VILLAGE VOICE. *April 26, 1994*

"People think this is an easy team to coach. …it's not that easy. Phil is the best coach in the world."

Michael Jordan had this to say about his coach in a 1996 ASSOCIATED PRESS report.

·5·

There's No One Like Mike

JACKSON DOESN'T HIDE
the fact that he's made champions of the
Chicago Bulls with the undeniable winning
spirit and supreme basketball talent of
Michael Jordan. He admits being in awe of
Jordan's ability when he joined the team as
an assistant. But in searching for ways to
improve the team, he wasn't afraid to tinker
with the superstar's role in the offense.

"...[*Michael Jordan is a*] one-man wreck-

ing crew, the greatest luxury a coach

could ever have."

NEW YORK TIMES MAGAZINE. *May 17, 1992*

"If Sylvester Stallone is getting $20 million

a movie, I can't imagine why Michael

doesn't get $20 million for a season."

CHICAGO TRIBUNE. *June 18, 1996*

"My first concern when I got the job was trying to treat Michael as equally as possible on the court. That's what our offensive system is all about. But there is no possible way to treat him like every other player off the floor....There is a difference in the way he's treated, yes, but there's also a difference in the way he produces. A big difference."

SPORTS ILLUSTRATED. *November 11, 1991*

"The greatness of Michael Jordan is his competitive drive; the weakness of Michael Jordan is his competitive drive."

NEW YORK TIMES MAGAZINE. *May 17, 1992*

"Sometimes
he keeps things
moving by not
doing anything.
With Phil
there's a
flowing rather
than a forcing."

June Jackson weighed in
on her husband in a 1992 feature
in NEW YORK TIMES MAGAZINE.

•6•

Fatal Distractions

WITH ANY COACHING POST comes the everyday distractions of running a big-time basketball outfit. There's personnel problems, cranky referees, abusive opponents, and other annoyances that perpetually threaten to trigger an unraveling. In mastering a comfortable balance, Jackson's been able to enjoy the long, precious ride.

"...It's very easy to become distracted in this game, particularly when there is a lot of adulation and following that goes your way. So we're trying to keep our focus. We're trying to keep the major things we do, our practices and relative pregame and postgame things, the same to keep everything on key. We have very little control of our environment. But we can control some of that environment and that's the best we can do."

THE SPORTING NEWS. *November 11, 1991*

"Sometimes you get home and you get lethargic because you know how easy it is to win at home, especially with the momentum we've built up on our court."

CHICAGO SUN-TIMES. *March 4, 1997*

"Our enemy is ourselves, no doubt. When you have a talented team, your enemy is overconfidence or a lackadaisical attitude. You have to keep finding challenges. That is what ultimately drove Michael out of the game after we won three championships..."

CHICAGO TRIBUNE. *September 25, 1996*

[*On his hippie days*] "Put it this way; if you never tried anything, you weren't really participating in your generation."

US NEWS AND WORLD REPORT. *May 11, 1992*

"So many things have to happen for us to be beaten on a certain night. Michael has to have a bad night. Scottie's got to have a bad night and Dennis has to be either thrown out or suspended. You know all of those things probably aren't going to happen on the same night."

CHICAGO TRIBUNE. *March 12, 1997*

"I do realize the reality of the situation and sometimes I pinch myself to make sure it's happening....I realize it doesn't happen that often in a coach's career and I try to make sure I enjoy it."

WGN-TV. *February 11, 1997*

[*On coaching what might be the greatest team ever*] "You really can't compare generations. It's difficult to say this decade or that or this group or that group is the greatest. This [*Bulls*] team right now is the greatest because it's playing right now. We're simply the best at this point in time."

CHICAGO TRIBUNE. *April 17, 1996*

"There's a part of me that revels in the joy of what's happened. There's also a part of me that in the past would have been waiting for the other shoe to drop. 'I've had success, but now failure must follow.' That's a very human trait, that fear of failure creeping up behind us. And the fortunate thing for me in this coaching career is that I've not only enjoyed the success that has happened to us, but I'm no longer worried about the next step and the failure or the losing to come. I know there's a balance in my life."

INC. ONLINE. *June 13, 1996*

"He'll give Dennis space as long as Dennis knows he has to play with the rest of the team."

Bulls guard Steve Kerr assessed the Rodman approach in a 1996 article in SPORTS ILLUSTRATED

•7•

And Along Came Dennis

TALK ABOUT DISTRACTIONS.
Who could prepare to coach the reigning bad-
boy of basketball — two-toned hair, tattoo-
covered body, on-the-court antics, and one of
the greatest rebounders ever. With his own
rebellious streak behind him and his keen
ability to relate to most anyone, Jackson was
ready and willing to take a chance on the man
everyone was trying to forget. Only kicks and
head-butts could sour the coach's enthusiasm
over acquiring this Worm of a player.

"We needed a player we could put on the floor with Michael and Scottie and the rest of the starting team every night — someone they could go to war with. This was the guy who fit that package perfectly."

BECKETT PROFILES, *1996*

"Dennis knows how to play basketball. He's got a real sense for the game and a flair for the dramatics. He brings a lot of energy to the game. That's really what we like about him — the fact that he throws himself around and he will generate energy in the ball game."

CHICAGO TRIBUNE. *October 14, 1995*

"Dennis is going to get that basketball at the cost of pulling it away from his team-mate sometimes. It's a magnetism for him. I've never seen anybody with the desire to get rebounds and loose balls the way Dennis does."

CHICAGO TRIBUNE. *February 29, 1996*

"I come from a more Puritan background, a fundamentalist family and Montana, a provincial state. But as a child I did get a chance to do a lot of things that were unusual and different. So I had a lot of flexibility where I grew up. I was taught to always keep an open mind and keep a compassionate heart. From that standpoint, my parents gave me some of the necessary equipment to do this job. Understanding people and where they come from is one of the things my father was very good at."

THE SPORTING NEWS. *October 16, 1995*

"Dennis will always be at the edge. But

I don't feel he has to be more shocking

each time…"

CHICAGO TRIBUNE. *September 25, 1996*

"Dennis Rodman brings a lot of levity to the team….Dennis does a lot of things that we think are funny and we try to use those things to our advantage rather than getting upset about them."

SAN ANTONIO EXPRESS-NEWS. *February 11, 1996*

"I still think
he could
go back
and be
governor of
North Dakota."

**That's the forcecast Jackson's former
coach Red Holzman suggested to
SPORTS ILLUSTRATED in 1991.**

· 8 ·

Life Beyond the Game

FOR THOSE WHO WERE SURPRISED
Jackson made a career of coaching, he may
surprise them yet again if he chooses to re-
sign with the Bulls for the 1997-98 season,
which would be his eighth year as head
coach. Still, Jackson sees coaching as just
one facet of his life. What he'll do next is
still unclear. But the Zen master is always
searching, always thinking, always winning.

"The real point is what's happening with the people you're touching — with your family, first of all, and your job and community. There's a tornado of events that sweeps you up and then touches you down in a certain spot in time. What's the reason? What's to be gained from a human standpoint? Am I contributing? Or am I detracting?"

NEW YORK TIMES MAGAZINE. *May 17, 1992*

"There's nothing we'd rather do than go out and win another championship and then walk away. What better feeling to finish in a professional situation than a run of eight, nine years for me and 12 or 13 for [*Jordan*]."

CHICAGO TRIBUNE. *September 25, 1996*

"Well, I do want to do something worthwhile after basketball, but I'm just not sure what it is. Everything comes with a price....But I've got time. I'll study my options."

SPORTS ILLUSTRATED. *November 11, 1991*